T0406031

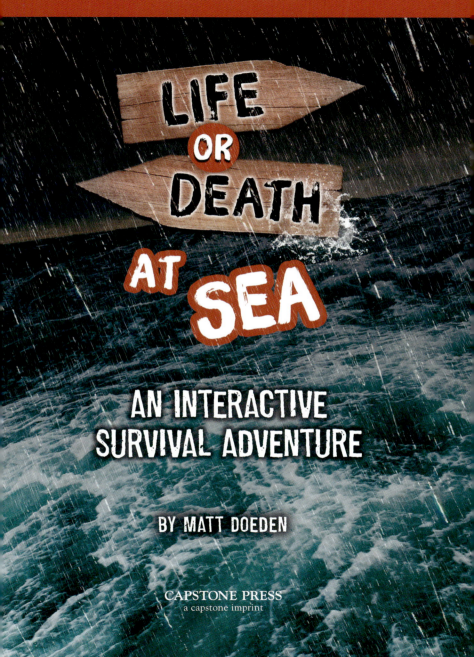

LIFE OR DEATH AT SEA

AN INTERACTIVE SURVIVAL ADVENTURE

BY MATT DOEDEN

CAPSTONE PRESS
a capstone imprint

Published by Capstone Press, an imprint of Capstone
1710 Roe Crest Drive, North Mankato, Minnesota 56003
capstonepub.com

Copyright © 2025 by Capstone. All rights reserved. No part of this publication may
be reproduced in whole or in part, or stored in a retrieval system, or transmitted
in any form or by any means, electronic, mechanical, photocopying, recording, or
otherwise, without written permission of the publisher.

Library of Congress Cataloging-in-Publication Data is available on the Library of
Congress website.

ISBN: 9781669088332 (hardcover)
ISBN: 9781669088301 (paperback)
ISBN: 9781669088318 (ebook PDF)

Summary: Readers face the challenges of being lost at sea, inspired by the
experiences of real people.

Editorial Credits
Editor: Mandy Robbins; Designer: Dina Her; Media Researcher: Jo Miller;
Production Specialist: Tori Abraham

Image Credits:
Getty Images: AFP, 107, Carlos Gotay, 19, Christophe Lehenaff, 30, Ippei Naoi,
37, Jack Paylor, 94, jcrosemann, 46, Merche Portu, 26; Shutterstock: Aastels, 38,
andrejs polivanovs, 4, Artens, 64, BROTEstudio, 72, daren horwood, 83, Dziegler,
67, ESB Professional, 100, haveseen, 78, Ivan Cholakov, 40, Kathy Hutchins, 107,
mapush, 50, Petr Jilek, 88, photka, 28, Photomarine, 10, S. Hanusch, 55, sittitap, 8,
Stock High angle view, 71, YRABOTA, 6, ZHMURCHAK, cover, 1; Wikimedia:
U.S.Army, 106

Design Elements:
Shutterstock: ecco, feelphoto2521, Here, oxinoxi, railway fx

Any additional websites and resources referenced in this book are not maintained,
authorized, or sponsored by Capstone. All product and company names are
trademarks™ or registered® trademarks of their respective holders.

Printed and bound in the USA. 6121

TABLE OF CONTENTS

ABOUT YOUR ADVENTURE

YOU are lost at sea. With few resources and no help, you're adrift on the open ocean. Threats are everywhere. Hunger . . . thirst . . . storms . . . sharks. It's a constant struggle just to live through another day. YOU CHOOSE what path to take. Will you sink, or will you swim?

Turn the page to begin your adventure.

CHAPTER 1

ADRIFT

The ocean is still. The deep blue water is all that you can see in every direction. You always knew that the ocean was vast. But you never really understood what that meant—until now.

It wasn't supposed to be like this. A simple journey turned horribly wrong in an instant. Now, you're cast adrift, with little hope of rescue. You're at the mercy of the sea, and the sea is harsh and unforgiving.

Turn the page.

You look up. More blue hangs above you, with just a few wispy white clouds. You scan the sky for signs of life. A flock of seagulls might hint at nearby land. But there is nothing. Well . . . not quite nothing. Far to the west, darker clouds trace the horizon. A storm is building.

You shudder at the thought of lightning, thunder, howling winds, and crashing waves. Every day—every hour—is a nonstop battle just to stay alive. If the storm comes your way, you don't know if you'll have what it takes to make it through. Out here, nothing is safe. You'll need to stay strong, keep calm, and get a little lucky to make it through this alive.

You remind yourself to be brave. But you can't help but ask yourself, "How did I wind up here?"

- To sail the Pacific with friends, turn to page 11.

- To fly from Fiji to Guam on a turboprop airplane touring the South Pacific, turn to page 41.

- To take a day trip on a fishing boat during your vacation, turn to page 73.

CHAPTER 2

EYE OF THE STORM

Maya leans over the railing at the bow of your little sailboat.

"Woooooo!" she shouts as waves slap against the hull.

You shake your head and smile. You've been out here for four days, but she still spends hours staring down at the water.

"Looking for dolphins again?" you ask.

Maya turns and nods. "I'm going to spot some before this trip is over. You'll see."

Turn the page.

It's a running joke between the two of you. You are best friends on a trip from California to Hawaii.

You've sailed all your life. The forty-foot sailboat is named *Summer*. Its owner hired you to sail it to Honolulu. The job doesn't pay much, but you'd have done it for free. It's the sort of adventure you've always wanted to take.

The first four days go smoothly. But on day eight, about halfway through your journey, that changes. The calm ocean breeze becomes gusty, and the sea grows rougher by the hour. You and Maya stand on the deck, looking at the threatening sky. Heavy dark clouds hang over the horizon to the west—right in the direction you're sailing.

"Do you know how to sail through a storm?" Maya asks, a little panic creeping into her voice.

The idea of a storm on the open ocean scares you as well. But you don't want to alarm her.

"Ships go through storms all the time," you say. "The ride might be a little rocky, but we'll be fine. It might not even hit us."

You really wish the boat was in better condition. It's showing its age. The sails are tattered. The long-range radio doesn't work. It's perfectly seaworthy. But it's an old boat.

Turn the page.

In the late afternoon, the storm arrives. It starts with a powerful gust of wind. You lower your normal sails and raise the much smaller storm sails. The full-size sails are a danger in strong winds. They could tear or catch too much wind and make the boat impossible to steer. Driving rain begins to fall, and the water churns with big waves.

You remember all you've learned. You steer directly into the waves. If they hit the side of the boat, they could tip it over. Your stomach feels sick as the little craft rocks up and down.

The storm grows stronger by the minute. You can barely steer through the growing waves. The hull creaks and groans at the stress. You clench the ship's wheel so hard that your knuckles turn white.

Maya comes up out of the cabin below. You shout at her to stay down, but she can't hear you over the wind, rain, and thunder. As she rushes toward the railing, you realize she's going to throw up.

"Maya, no!" you shout.

Just then, a huge wave swells. A gust of wind turns the boat slightly, leaving the broadside of your hull exposed to the wave. It hits with terrible force. You grip the wheel, desperately trying to keep control.

When you look back toward your friend, the deck is empty. Your hands go limp as you realize what has happened. Maya has been washed overboard. You frantically scan the water for a sign of her. "Maya!" you shout, but you can barely hear your own voice over the raging storm.

- To rush to the railing to try to spot Maya, turn to page 16.
- To stay here and hold on tight, turn to page 18.

You have to try to find your friend. You stumble to the railing and scan the water.

"Maya!" you shout again. But the water looks almost black under the dark clouds. Waves rock the boat back and forth violently. Panic wells up in your chest. The wind hits you, almost knocking you over. The rain stings your face. For a moment, you spot a shape. Is it Maya?

A wave hits, almost sending you over the railing yourself. It's not safe out here. But what if there's a chance to save Maya? A life ring is attached to the railing near the prow. Should you risk your own safety to throw the ring to the shape you hope is Maya?

- To go back to the ship's wheel and try to keep her afloat, go to the next page.
- To go for the life ring, turn to page 26.

Your instinct to survive overwhelms your urge to save your friend. You doubt you could make it to the life ring and back without falling overboard. It's hopeless. You'll never see Maya in the dark, churning waves. And you might lose your own life trying.

Another wave slams into the boat. It flings you to the deck. You must get back to the wheel. You are exhausted and heartbroken, but your survival instinct propels you. You crawl back and hold on for your life. It's all you can do.

You grip the wheel tightly as the boat rocks and scan continuously for your friend. You hope to see her pop up out of the angry waters, but she's gone. With the crash of a wave, you've lost your best friend.

Turn the page.

For another half hour, you hold on with all your might. The boat creaks. You hear wood snap. But the boat makes it through. Soon, the sky brightens. The wind dies down, and the water grows calmer.

You've made it. But the storm has come at a terrible price. Your friend is gone. The boat is in ruins. The mast has snapped in half. The rudder is broken. You're alone and adrift in the middle of the Pacific with no way to call for help.

Exhausted, you flop down on one of the cots belowdecks. Your mind goes back to the sounds you heard during the storm—the snapping of wood. You should really check the boat for damage. But you're exhausted and in despair. You just want to sleep.

The sun is setting. You don't have much daylight left. Should you check the boat with the little light you have left or rest and check it tomorrow?

- To check the boat, turn to page 20.
- To go to sleep, turn to page 22.

Your whole body hurts. Your heart is broken. But it's not the time to rest. This is an old boat, and that was some rough sailing.

A quick walk on the deck shows the damage. The mast is broken. That means you won't be able to use a proper sail. But the bigger problem lies below. A thin crack runs along the hull, just inches above the waterline. A crack like that will leak and cause the boat to sink. You have to repair it now while there's still light.

Luckily, you have the supplies—a tube of sealant and a roll of waterproof tape. You climb down and dry the area and squeeze the sealant into the crack. Next, you tear off long strips of the tape and carefully cover the crack. It's a temporary fix. It won't stop the crack from growing in rough waters. But it will stop the leak for now.

You spend the next three days drifting. The wind and currents are pulling you southwest. You think you might be in the California Current. That would take you south, farther from Hawaii, before circling back north, toward the islands. It would be a long voyage, but you would get where you need to go.

On the other hand, if you can fashion some sort of sail, you could push north and get there quicker. It would be hard work, but you just might be able to do it.

- To let the current carry you, turn to page 34.
- To try to make a sail, turn to page 36.

You can't deal with anything more tonight. You close your eyes. You fall asleep almost instantly and slip into a deep sleep. Sometime in the middle of the night, you wake. At first, you're confused. It takes a moment to recall your situation. Then you hear it. Drip . . . drip . . . drip.

You leap out of bed. Your feet hit the floor with a splash. You're standing in several inches of cold ocean water. A leak!

You grab your flashlight and rush above decks. You shine the beam of light down on the hull below you.

That's when you see a long, thin crack in the hull, extending down below the waterline. You shudder. With every moment, more water leaks in. The boat is going down. Your only hope is to deploy the life raft. But you'll need food, water, and other supplies to survive on the raft. Do you have time to get them? The water is rising fast.

- To deploy the boat's small inflatable life raft, turn to page 24.
- To gather supplies first, turn to page 28.

You don't have time to run around the boat finding supplies. You just need to get the life raft. You rush to the back of the boat and pull it out of a trunk. You pull a pin, and the raft automatically inflates. It's only about six feet long.

Luckily, a handful of supplies are in the trunk too. You grab a small tarp, a whistle, a flare, two water bottles, and a small paddle.

The water is pouring in through the crack now. The rear of the boat is sinking. You carefully lower the raft over the railing. The ocean surface is just a foot or so below the deck now. You throw in your supplies and slide over the railing.

As you paddle away, the boat slips under the waves. Just like that, it's gone. You can hardly believe it.

You watch the sun rise from your little raft. Everywhere you look is flat, blue ocean. There's almost nothing between North America and Hawaii. And you're right between them. You know that there are several shipping lanes to the north. You could paddle that way and hope to run across a ship. But maybe it would be better to conserve your energy. You don't have any food.

- To start paddling, turn to page 30.
- To save your energy, turn to page 32.

You can't give up on your best friend.
Grasping the railing, you pull yourself forward
against the wind, inching closer to the ring.
Finally, you grab it.

You look back out at the water. It's dark.
You think you see something amongst the rain
and waves. It might be Maya. You let go of the
railing and use both hands to hurl the ring as far
as you can.

Just then, another wave slams into the boat. You lose your balance and fall forward, slamming your head onto the metal railing. The impact stuns you for a moment. The boat lurches as another wave hits, and you're tossed headfirst into the water.

You go under, then come up a few seconds later. You gasp for air and look for the life ring. You don't see it. You fight the waves and try to swim back, but it's hopeless. Your wet clothes weigh you down. The ocean pulls you down. The next time you go under, you don't come back up.

THE END

To follow another path, turn to page 9.
To learn more about survival at sea, turn to page 101.

In a panic, you rush to gather what you can before the boat sinks. You grab your backpack from belowdecks and fill it with water bottles and canned food. You toss in extra clothes, a lighter, and a knife for cleaning fish.

You can feel the boat leaning heavily to one side. The water pouring in grows louder by the second. You hurry above decks and head to the back of the boat where the raft is packed in a trunk. In the darkness, it takes you a moment to realize it's already under the water.

You push into the water, wading ankle-deep, then knee-deep, then hip-deep. You feel for the chest frantically. After a moment, you find it. But in the cold water, your fingers are clumsy. You can't manage to unlatch the trunk. The boat tilts more and more as the rear slips into the water.

You're too late. The boat is going under, and you didn't get the life raft out in time. All you can do is swim as the water pulls the boat under the waves.

You might survive for a few hours out here, exposed and alone. But that won't be enough. Soon, you will join your friend Maya and be truly lost at sea.

THE END

To follow another path, turn to page 9.
To learn more about survival at sea, turn to page 101.

You can't just sit here and do nothing. You start to paddle. The raft is light, so you move with ease. You keep a slow, steady pace, taking breaks when you need them. By late morning, when the sun is strong, you rest under the tarp. As late afternoon arrives, you go back to paddling.

The stars are brilliant that night. You never knew there were so many. Your thoughts go back to Maya. You sob and wonder if you'll end up lost at sea like her. You alternate between fits of sleep and paddling, using the bright North Star as a guide.

You run out of water on the second day. Your time is running out. But you try to stay positive. You're too anxious to sleep that night. Luckily, you notice lights in the distance. It's a ship!

You quickly grab the whistle and your flashlight. You blow with all your might and frantically sweep the flashlight back and forth. For several minutes, the ship doesn't seem to notice you. The thought of it passing so close is almost too much to bear. You keep whistling.

Finally, the ship blares its horn. Someone has seen you! The ship turns slowly in your direction. Somehow, against all odds, you're going to make it. You only wish Maya was here with you.

THE END

To follow another path, turn to page 9.
To learn more about survival at sea, turn to page 101.

You look at your paddle. It's tiny. Your raft is tiny too. Out here in the endless ocean, paddling seems like a waste of energy. You'll let the currents take you where they will.

By noon, the sun is baking you. You hide under the tarp. You take little sips of water. Your supply won't last long. At one point, you see a large, dark shape move deep below you. It could be a whale—or a shark.

Day turns into night. There's no sign of any ships. You do spot one airplane high in the sky, but you have no way to signal for help.

You survive the day and endure the night. On the second day, you run out of water. The sun beats down on you. You're weak and dehydrated. The third day, you drift in and out of consciousness. No one is coming to help you. You know you won't survive a fourth day.

THE END

To follow another path, turn to page 9.

To learn more about survival at sea, turn to page 101.

What good could a little homemade sail really do? You'd just waste your energy and resources. You have food and water for two weeks. You must be smart and make it last. With a little luck, the currents will take you past an island.

Days pass. You try fishing, but you don't have any luck. At one point, you spot several sea birds on the horizon. It gives you hope that land is nearby. But you never see it.

Days turn into weeks. You're low on food. But water is the bigger problem. Your bottled water is almost gone. You've captured a little fresh water during brief rainstorms. But it's not enough.

Twenty days after the storm, you're dehydrated and hungry. You barely have the energy to stand up. That's when your quick fix of the hull begins to fail. The boat is taking on water again, and you're too weak to do anything about it.

The boat sits lower and lower in the endless expanse of blue. Soon, it will sink, and it will take you with it.

THE END

To follow another path, turn to page 9.
To learn more about survival at sea, turn to page 101.

The key to survival is to never stop trying. You want to give yourself every chance. You cut a six-foot piece of the main sail and tie each end to the broken mast. It's an ugly, inefficient sail. But it does catch some wind, and you're able to point yourself north.

Sometimes, it seems like you're barely moving, but you stick with it. You hold that northerly heading day after day. Two weeks pass. You're low on food and water, so you decrease your rations. You still have hope. You won't give up.

Sometimes, doubts creep in. What if you don't find land? There are times you just feel like giving in. But you won't let yourself.

After eighteen days, you spot a flock of sea birds. Your heart races. That many birds must mean land is nearby. You grab your binoculars and scan the horizon. To the northwest, you can just make out a hazy dark shape. It must be one of the Hawaiian Islands!

Turn the page.

You adjust the wheel and head straight for
it. A few hours later, a private yacht crosses your
path. The people aboard notice the condition of
your boat and head straight for you.

"Do you need help?" calls a young woman.

You can barely believe your luck as the yacht pulls alongside you. You're so overcome by emotion that you can barely answer. The woman helps you aboard the yacht and brings you a granola bar and a bottle of water.

"We'll have you back on land in no time," she says. "What a story you must have."

You nod, sadly, thinking of Maya.

THE END

To follow another path, turn to page 9.
To learn more about survival at sea, turn to page 101.

CHAPTER 3

BLOOD IN THE WATER

Seru's knuckles turn white as he grips the control stick of the small turboprop plane he's piloting.

"We're going down!" he shouts.

The words don't seem real. How did you get here? This morning, you were in Fiji, enjoying a trip through the South Pacific. On a whim, you hopped onto a plane with a stranger bound for Guam. For weeks, you've been going from island to island, staying wherever you can find a bed and surfing wherever you can find a wave.

Turn the page.

As the small plane falls toward the vast blue ocean, you realize that carefree trip is over. Your fingers dig into the fabric of your seat as Seru fights to keep the small twin-engine turboprop airplane level as it falls. The silence is almost as terrifying as the view. Both of the plane's engines have failed.

"There's an emergency life raft in the back," Seru tells you. "It's folded up in a plastic case. Grab it!"

In a haze, you unbuckle your seat belt and stumble into the back of the plane. You grab the bright orange raft and step back into the cockpit. You have just enough time to sit down and buckle back in before impact.

Seru is a skilled pilot. With no power, he guides the plane to as soft a water landing as possible, but it's still a jolt. Water splashes over the plane as it skids onto the ocean surface.

You both unbuckle and head for the exit. The plane is floating for the moment. But it's a matter of minutes before it's on its way to the ocean floor. With the raft in hand, you leap into the water. You turn to watch Seru follow. But he disappears back into the plane.

"I have some supplies!" he shouts back.

"No!" you call back. "Get out!"

Several seconds pass. The plane's nose dips ever lower into the ocean as it fills with water. The water is about to reach the open exit door. When it does, everything will go down fast.

Turn the page.

"Come on, Seru!" you shout.

At the last moment, he appears with a small backpack in hand. He stands at the exit door, struggling.

"My foot is caught," he says, panicked. "Something is wrapped around it. "Help me!"

If you don't help Seru, he's doomed. But if you do, you might get sucked down with the plane. Should you risk your own life to try to save Seru's?

- To help Seru, go to the next page.
- To stay away from the sinking plane, turn to page 48.

You won't leave someone struggling like that. You swim back to the plane. A thin cord is wrapped around Seru's ankle. As you pull on the cord, water pours in through the open exit door. The plane creaks and groans as the water pulls it down.

The cord is tight, so you think fast. You quickly grab Seru's shoe and yank it off his foot. Then you slide the cord down around his heel and off of his foot. He's free!

The two of you push off from the doorway just as the plane begins to sink. As it goes down, it sucks you with it. You swim as hard as you can against the strong force. For a moment, it seems helpless. But you slowly make your way back to the surface. You gasp for breath. A few feet away, Seru comes up and does the same.

Turn the page.

Somehow, you held on to the raft. You pull on the small cord, which releases compressed gas into the raft. In seconds, the bright orange raft is floating on the surface. You both get in. It's barely big enough for both of you. But for the moment, it's all that's keeping you alive.

When the shock of the crash wears off, the reality of your situation hits. You're alive. But for how long? Seru grabbed some water bottles and two bags of trail mix, along with a few tools. He also took a second raft. It's all you have out here on what feels like endless ocean.

You sit in silence for a while. Both of you are trying to process what just happened—and what happens next. You're constantly bumping into each other. The raft is so small that neither of you can do anything but sit cross-legged.

"Maybe we should inflate the second raft," you say. "We could tie them together and have twice as much room."

"Or should we save it in case something happens to this one?" Seru asks.

- To inflate the second raft, turn to page 54.
- To save it for an emergency, turn to page 56.

You freeze. After the terror of the violent water landing, you're too afraid to put yourself back in danger.

Seru calls out, "Help! Help me, please!"

Stuck in fear, you watch as the water drags the plane down, taking Seru with it. You know you'll live with that guilt the rest of your life—however long that may be.

The raft has a small cord that you pull. Compressed air fills it. In seconds, it's floating. You climb in and look around. Only a small oil slick remains of the airplane.

You spend the rest of the day and that night floating. You have no food, water, or supplies, just a small patch kit tucked into the back of the raft.

A brief rain shower passes over at dawn. You collect what water you can in the plastic sleeve that held the raft. It's something, but it won't last long.

You doze off the next afternoon, but you're awakened by a sudden jolt. Startled, you look around, but you see nothing.

THUD! There it is again! Something just hit your raft from below. You look over the edge and see a dark shape in the water. Shark!

Your heart pounds. You can hardly believe this is real. How much worse could your luck get?

Turn the page.

The shark swims a large circle and comes again. Its body slides against the raft. Then, you hear a sickening hissing sound. The shark has punctured the raft, just below the waterline on the left side. Air is escaping out of a small slit.

What do you do? To patch the raft, you'll have to get into the water—with a shark. But the raft will sink if it loses too much air.

- To get into the water to patch the raft, go to the next page.
- To remain in the raft until the shark leaves, turn to page 60.

If the raft deflates, you'll be in the water anyway. You must act quickly. You grab the patch kit and slip quietly over the edge into the water. You do your best not to make a splash.

You lift the corner of the raft and get to work. It's a simple job, but your fear makes you sloppy. You almost drop the patch into the water, but you collect yourself and stick it on. The leaking stops. You let out a breath and try to pull yourself back into the raft.

It's harder than you thought it would be. Your hands slip on the smooth, wet surface of the raft, and you tumble back into the water with a splash. You can see the shark approaching—fast. It's coming straight at you. You only have a second or two to act.

- To kick the shark as it approaches, turn to page 52.
- To try to pull yourself up again, turn to page 62.

You grab tightly to the edge of the raft to brace yourself. As the shark charges, you tuck your knees in. Then, just as it arrives, you kick as hard as you can. Both feet slam into the predator's nose as it comes in to take a bite. The kick seems to stun the shark. It veers off to your left and swims away.

You pull yourself up and collapse inside the raft. You breathe deeply to calm yourself. More than ever, you know it will be a constant battle for your life out here.

For three days, you do all you can to stay alive. You catch water with every rain shower. Your stomach rumbles from the lack of food.

Early on the fourth day, several sea birds appear in the sky. They seem curious about you. They swoop overhead—almost within reach. If you could leap at one, you might just catch it. But doing that would probably cause you to fall into the water. After your shark encounter, the idea of going back into the ocean is terrifying.

- To stay safe inside the raft, turn to page 59.
- To try to catch a bird, turn to page 64.

"I think we need them both now," you say.

Seru agrees and pulls the cord on the second raft. Soon, you're each feeling much more comfortable in your own rafts. You use a strap from Seru's backpack to bind the rafts together.

The first day and night, you're pretty quiet. You're both thinking about your dire situation. A brief rain shower in the morning allows you to collect some water. You'll need every drop you can get. By that afternoon, the two of you chat to pass the time. You're very glad you're not alone out here.

But the good feelings don't last long. Late in the afternoon, the wind picks up. The water gets choppy. As the rafts roll up and down the waves, the strap breaks loose. Suddenly, you're separated.

Panic sets in as Seru's raft floats twenty feet away . . . thirty feet. You're going to lose each other! You look at the water. It's rough, but you could probably swim it. Is it worth the risk to try to reconnect the rafts?

- To stay in your raft, turn to page 58.
- To dive into the water and try to pull your raft to Seru's, turn to page 66.

"We have to be smart," you say. "We might need that later."

Seru sighs. "You're right. We'll hold on to it, just in case."

For three days and nights, the two of you are crammed together in the small raft. You catch rainwater and eat just a bit of trail mix each day. Luckily, the raft's tarp roof gives you shelter from the intense sun.

On the fifth day, a small shark rams into the raft. Its fin punctures the raft and air begins to escape. You're relieved to have the other raft. You quickly inflate it and climb in. From there, you patch the punctured raft. You tie the two together with a strap from Seru's backpack.

Another week passes. You're barely hanging on. Seru is fading fast. He sleeps most of the time, and he mumbles nonsense when he's awake. You fear he doesn't have long left. And neither do you. It hasn't rained in two days, and you're parched.

That night, you spot an island in the distance. You lean over the raft and paddle with your hands. It grows closer and closer. But the current is going to take you past it.

Seru is sleeping, and no matter what you do, he won't wake up. His breathing is shallow.

You could swim for the island. You think you could make it, but that would mean abandoning Seru. Can you do that after all you've been through together?

- To leave Seru and swim for the island, turn to page 67.
- To stay with Seru and hope someone spots you, turn to page 69.

"Seru!" you shout.

He calls back to you. Already, he's so far away that you can't make out what he's saying. You watch as the wind and waves carry him away. Finally, you lose sight of him. Now, you're truly alone.

Days pass. You survive on what little rainwater falls. A bag of trail mix is all the food you have, so you eat just a few handfuls each day. The raft's tarp roof protects your skin from the beating sun, but you're so thirsty. You don't know how much longer you can hold on.

A week after the crash, you spot something in the distance. It's an island! You watch it as the current carries you closer. But it soon becomes clear that you'll drift right past it. It's time to act.

Turn to page 63.

You can survive weeks without food. You won't survive minutes if another shark is waiting in the water below. So you watch the birds swoop and dive. A few minutes later, they move on. Again, you're alone in the middle of the ocean.

The next day, you're weak from hunger, and now you're out of water. You're so thirsty. You can't go on much longer. That's when you see it—an island in the distance. You have to get there. So you lean out over the water and start to paddle.

At first, it seems like you're standing still. But over the next few hours, you make slow progress. The island gets closer and closer. But you realize that you won't make it. The current will take you right past the island.

Turn to page 63.

There's no way you're going into the water with a shark. Maybe if you sit here quietly, it will swim away. Then you can patch the raft and refill it with your lungs. Your hands tremble as you scan the water, dreading another charge.

At first, you think you're in luck. The shark doesn't charge again. You can still see the shadow under the water. But it's not attacking.

The firm body of the raft begins to soften and crumple. You sit lower and lower in the water. You keep watching the shark, silently begging it to just leave. But it doesn't.

Air keeps escaping. Soon, water pours over a deflated corner of the raft. It's no longer strong enough to hold you. Everything slips into the water—including you.

Too late, you realize your mistake. The dark shape is coming. And there's nowhere for you to hide.

THE END

To follow another path, turn to page 9.
To learn more about survival at sea, turn to page 101.

You grab the edge of the raft and pull yourself up with all of your strength. But the raft is too slippery. Your fingers can't grip it.

The shark attacks with vicious force. Its jaws clamp down on your left leg. You thrash and kick, and after a few moments, it lets go.

The water around you is stained red with your blood. That's when a second shark hits. It slams into your side and drags you under the water. That's just enough time for you to see more dark shapes lurking in the depths. You're wounded. You're exhausted. Your raft is now out of reach. This is the end.

THE END

To follow another path, turn to page 9.
To learn more about survival at sea, turn to page 101.

You only have one chance. You must swim for it. It's a long distance, but you're a strong swimmer. You jump in and start to swim.

The hope of rescue gives you a burst of energy. You stroke and kick with everything you have—and you're making real progress.

But the adrenaline wears off quickly. You're starving and dehydrated. Your legs cramp up, and you cry out in pain. Your body doesn't have the strength to make it to the island. Your head dips under the surface, and salty seawater fills your lungs.

You were so close. You just aren't going to make it.

THE END

To follow another path, turn to page 9.
To learn more about survival at sea, turn to page 101.

You are getting weaker by the hour. You need food. You slowly stand up. Your legs shake as you wait for a bird. Finally, one swoops low. You launch yourself toward it. Somehow, you get it!

It's an incredible stroke of luck. With no fire, you have to eat the bird raw. You gulp down every scrap of meat. It's not a lot, but it's much-needed fuel for your body.

The next day, you spot an island in the distance. The current pulls you closer, but it's still several miles away. You don't hesitate. You might not get another chance. You jump in the water and start to swim. It takes every shred of energy you have, but you make it! You pull yourself up onto a rocky beach.

As you sit there, panting for breath, you hear a sound that's music to your ears. It's a car. There must be a road nearby!

You feel guilty that you survived while Seru didn't. You'll never forget those terrible days at sea. But you made it.

THE END

To follow another path, turn to page 9.
To learn more about survival at sea, turn to page 101.

The thought of being alone terrifies you, so you jump into the choppy water and try to swim toward Seru. You do all you can to drag your own raft behind you, but a wave knocks it out of your grasp. The light raft catches the wind and blows out of reach.

As you try to tread water, you realize you've made a horrible mistake. Your raft is gone. And with every second, Seru gets farther out of reach. Soon, he's just a small orange speck on the horizon.

You're alone, in the ocean, with no hope of rescue. You may survive an hour. Or two. But soon, you'll be truly lost at sea.

THE END

To follow another path, turn to page 9.
To learn more about survival at sea, turn to page 101.

It breaks your heart, but you can't miss what is likely to be your only chance to make it out alive. You take Seru's hand and tell him you're going for help. Then you slip overboard into the warm Pacific water.

Turn the page.

It's a long, hard swim. After about an hour, you make it. Lights dot the shore—homes. Your legs feel like jelly as you walk for the first time in more than a week. You knock on the front door of the nearest house. An elderly couple greets you and immediately sees that you're in desperate need of help.

Later that night, in the hospital, a police officer visits your room. "We sent boats out to search for your friend. No one has spotted him yet."

You close your eyes. You only knew Seru for a short time. But in that time, he was the most important person in your world. You hope against hope that they find him.

THE END

To follow another path, turn to page 9.
To learn more about survival at sea, turn to page 101.

You can't leave Seru now. Instead, you take off your shirt and wave it in the air. Maybe someone will see it.

An hour passes. Your arm aches from waving your shirt, but you keep going. You shout, whistle, and clap. But the current just keeps dragging you along. Slowly, the island grows farther and farther away. You can feel rescue slipping away.

Then you hear a faint sound—a motor! A small fishing boat appears on the horizon. It's headed straight for you.

"Hello," calls out a voice as the boat pulls alongside your rafts. "Are you okay?"

Turn the page.

Tears well up in your eyes. "Help," is all you can manage to get out as you begin to sob.

A young man lowers a small ladder and helps you up.

"Let's get you two to a hospital," he says. "You don't know how lucky you are we spotted you."

But you do know. You can hardly believe you're going to make it. And with medical help, hopefully, Seru will too.

THE END

To follow another path, turn to page 9.
To learn more about survival at sea, turn to page 101.

CHAPTER 4

LOST AND ALONE

"Let's go," the captain calls out. "I can tell the fish will be biting today."

He's a weathered old man who just goes by Cap—short for Captain. You smile as you step aboard the small, wooden fishing boat. Deep-sea fishing rigs line the dock. It was supposed to be a deep-sea fishing vacation in Ixtapa, Mexico, along the Pacific coast, for you and your brother. But he felt ill this morning. So now, it's just you, Cap, and a young couple on their honeymoon.

Turn the page.

The boat skips over the waves as Cap takes you far out to sea.

"I know where the sailfish are," he calls out from the helm. "You'll all go home with a fine trophy!"

You spend the afternoon fishing. Cap knows his stuff. You catch a huge sailfish and a smaller snapper. Jack and Maria—the young couple—catch a few as well. As the sun dips toward the horizon, Cap pats you on the back.

"It was a good day," he says with a grin. "But it's time to head back."

That's when the trouble begins. When Cap tries to start the motor, it gives a loud *POP*. A cloud of black smoke rises from the engine compartment.

Luckily, the boat has a much smaller second motor. Cap fires it up, but it's slow going. The small motor can barely keep up with the wind that wants to carry you back out to sea.

As sunset approaches, dark clouds roll in, and the wind begins to blow stronger and stronger. The waves grow larger. The boat rocks violently as Cap tries to keep it steady.

Suddenly, a massive wave hits. The little boat is tossed up and then sharply back down. Maria slips and slides down the wet deck. She grabs onto the railing as her body hangs over the edge. Cap rushes out to help. He grabs her by the arm, but another wave hits. You cling to a rope as the boat is tossed. When you look back up, Cap and Maria are gone. Jack screams, but he doesn't let go. Both of you are horrified.

Turn the page.

With Cap overboard, you do the only thing you can. You rush into the cockpit and take the wheel. You don't know much about steering a boat, even in good conditions. But you know that pointing the boat into the waves is your best chance. That way, it won't roll over and capsize.

For almost an hour, you battle the storm. Finally, the wind dies down. The waters calm. But the damage is done.

You're out of gas—adrift and being carried farther out to sea with every minute. You try to call for help on the ship's shortwave radio, but you get only static back.

Jack is crushed by the loss of Maria. He won't even get up to help collect supplies. For the first few days, he barely moves.

You take stock of supplies. You have a few cases of bottled water and soda. There's no food, but you have fish and enough gear to catch more when you need it. You don't have any way to cook the fish, so you just cut it up and eat it raw. But Jack refuses to eat anything.

"All we have to do is hang on until a ship spots us," you tell Jack. He just grunts. "Please eat something. You need food."

Jack acts like he doesn't even hear you. Without Maria, his will to live is weak.

Turn the page.

Weeks pass. Jack grows thinner and weaker. He finally does try some of the fish, but he can't keep it down. He's not going to last much longer out here.

You keep a constant watch for ships—but all you see is an endless expanse of blue. You could be hundreds of miles from land by now.

After about a month, you're losing hope. That's when you spot an island.

"Get up, Jack!" you shout. "It's an island. We have to try to get there. We can use the boat's inflatable life raft and paddle. Come on!"

But Jack is so weak and heartbroken, he's beyond caring. He won't move, and you can't carry him. Do you stay with him or take the chance to reach land?

- To stay with Jack, turn to page 80.
- To try to make it to the island, turn to page 82.

You hesitate. As badly as you want to go, you can't just abandon Jack. You'd never forgive yourself. You watch as the island slowly disappears over the horizon. Once again, all you see is blue water in every direction.

You keep trying to make Jack eat, but he can't keep anything down. He dies a few days later. You say a few words and then bury him at sea. Now, you're truly alone.

The weeks stretch on. Day after day is the same. Fish are plentiful, but your supply of bottled water runs out. You survive by catching what rain falls. But eventually, you run out.

After two days without water, you're badly dehydrated. You must drink something. Maybe just a little bit of ocean water would help you last until you get more rain.

You know you're not supposed to drink saltwater because it's too salty. But the only other fluid you have is your own urine. One way or another, you have to drink.

- To drink your own urine, turn to page 85.
- To drink a little ocean water, turn to page 91.

If Jack doesn't have the will to survive, you can't force him. But you won't let it take away your best chance at survival. You grab matches, a few water bottles, and some fishing gear. Then you lower the raft over the edge of the boat. You slide in and begin to paddle.

You watch for signs of people as you approach the island. But it looks deserted. It's small—no bigger than five or six city blocks. Dense forest covers most of it, with a small rocky peak at the center. You have no trouble paddling to a sandy beach on the island's south shore. You drag your raft up onto dry land and fall to your knees.

It's good to be on solid ground. But the island does turn out to be deserted. There are no buildings, roads, or any other signs that humans have ever been here.

You don't know how long you'll be stuck here, so you start building a shelter. It's a simple lean-to, made of small tree branches covered with leaves. It's not much, but it will keep you dry.

Next, you use dark rocks to spell out a big "SOS" on a white sand beach. If a plane flies overhead, maybe someone will spot it.

Turn the page.

The island becomes your home. You spend your days fishing, gathering edible plants, and collecting rainwater in large leaves. You spend hours each day on top of the rocky peak, searching the sea for signs of a ship or boat.

For the first few months, water isn't a problem. But then the rainfall patterns change. Days pass without rain. With nothing to drink, dehydration becomes a problem. You feel weak and dizzy. Your thirst is intense.

The only fresh water you know of is in a low-lying area of the island. But that water is stagnant and muddy. Who knows what kind of germs it could have. There's also a whole ocean of water right out there. Maybe you could drink a little. Just enough to wet your mouth.

- To drink the stagnant water, turn to page 87.
- To drink ocean water, turn to page 91.

Drinking sea water would just dehydrate you more. It would be deadly right now. As much as you hate the idea, you drink your own urine.

You choke down a few swallows. The taste almost makes you throw up, but you keep it down. It's disgusting, but it's enough to fight off dehydration for another day. And the next morning brings a hard rain shower. You fill several bottles with fresh water.

It was disgusting, but you're proud you were able to do what you had to do to last another day. The water you've collected now should last until the next rain. All you can do is stay sharp and hope for a lucky break.

Turn the page.

Weeks turn into months. One day, you see a ship in the distance. But it's too far away to signal. The shortwave radio's battery is long dead.

You feel like you may never see land again. The feeling of helplessness drives you into a deep depression. You must do something.

You don't know anything about motors. But maybe you could try to fix it. Or you could try to make a sail. You're not sure you're up for either task. But you have to do something to keep your mind from sinking lower.

- To try to fix the motor, turn to page 89.
- To try to make a sail, turn to page 90.

You know that drinking sea water can kill you. Maybe the stagnant water won't. You kneel down over the pool of water. It smells like mud and decomposing plant matter. You use an old water bottle to scoop some up. It's nasty.

You use your T-shirt as a filter. You double the fabric over a few times and drip the water through it. The water that comes out the other side is at least a little cleaner. But it still tastes awful. You drink just a little—enough to get you through another day. You're not sure you can do it again.

You're in luck. The next day, the rain finally returns. Once again, you have clean water to drink. You know you got lucky—that nasty water could have easily made you sick.

Turn the page.

Months pass. You find that you often speak out loud to yourself, just to hear a voice. It's lonely and a constant battle for survival. But you do what it takes.

After several months, you see something that almost seems too good to believe. A large container ship floats a few miles off of the island. This is your chance! You can signal the ship.

- To stand on the island's peak waving your shirt, turn to page 93.
- To start a big fire, turn to page 94.

The motor is in a compartment at the back of the boat. You open it up and look inside. Wires and tubes connect various parts. You have no idea what any of them do.

You start by making sure everything is connected tightly. You wiggle the moving parts. You turn the geared wheel. Then you try to start the engine. It makes a low whining sound, not the deep rumble of a motor starting.

You try again. Something clicks, and you hear a high-pitched screech, like metal rubbing metal. You smell gasoline. You're afraid that if you do start the motor, it could ignite the gas in the air and set the whole boat on fire.

"Hmm," you say out loud. "Not sure this is a very good idea."

- To keep trying, turn to page 96.
- To give up, turn to page 98.

There is a bedsheet on a small cot belowdecks. You've been sleeping on it, but now you have a better plan. You tie the sheet to the top of the boat, stretching it across to catch the wind. You have no way to adjust it. You can't steer the boat. You can only go where the wind takes you. But at least you're moving. Covering more territory improves your odds of coming across an island or another ship.

Two days later, a small storm hits. The winds rip your sail loose. Helplessly, you watch it fly away. You feel defeated. All of your work was for nothing. Maybe you should just give up and let the currents take you where they may.

- To give up on making a sail, turn to page 98.
- To try again, turn to page 99.

You're so thirsty, you ignore common sense. You scoop up some ocean water in your palms and drink it.

The powerful saltiness makes you cough and wretch. But you force a little down. Just a few sips. Any kind of water has to be better than nothing . . . right?

Soon, you realize you've made a terrible mistake. The salt in the water is dehydrating you even faster. Your stomach churns. You may throw up. You lie down for a few minutes, exhausted. When you try to stand up, you feel dizzy and faint.

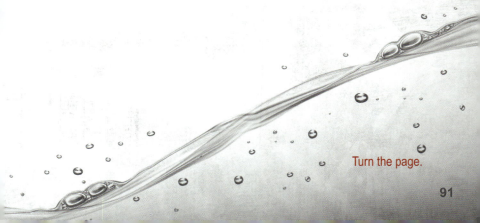

Turn the page.

It's a hard fall, and you hit your head on something sharp. As you drift in and out of consciousness, you taste blood in your mouth.

You made a fatal mistake. Now, dehydration is causing your organs to shut down. Even if rescue arrived right now, it would be too late. You survived months lost at sea. But it wasn't long enough.

THE END

To follow another path, turn to page 9.
To learn more about survival at sea, turn to page 101.

You scramble up the rocky peak as fast as you can. You stand at the top and wave your shirt back and forth. You shout and jump with all your might in hopes someone will notice.

But no one does. Your heart sinks when the big ship chugs away. As it disappears out of sight, you break down in tears. You were so close!

Just like that, it's back to daily life on your little island. You'll keep doing what you can to live another day . . . a week . . . a month. You have to believe that wasn't your only chance at rescue. Maybe next time, you'll find another way.

THE END

To follow another path, turn to page 9.
To learn more about survival at sea, turn to page 101.

Quickly, you bring all the firewood you have collected to the beach. It is directly in the ship's line of sight. You light the fire and feed it every piece of wood you can find. Soon, the blaze is taller than you. A line of dark gray smoke curls up into the sky.

You watch the ship desperately. It doesn't seem to be moving. But then you see a smaller boat speeding to the island. They saw your fire!

As the boat reaches shore, two men hop out and call to you in Chinese. You don't understand them, and they don't understand you. But your situation is clear, and they invite you onto their boat. On board, they feed you, give you fresh clothes, and take you to the captain. Nobody speaks English, but you do make out one word—Peru. It must be where they're headed, and they're taking you along.

You made it. After almost a year lost at sea, your family and friends probably think you're dead. Boy, are they in for a surprise!

THE END

To follow another path, turn to page 9.
To learn more about survival at sea, turn to page 101.

A fire would be bad. But it's worth the risk. You keep tinkering with the motor. You figure out how to pull out the spark plugs. A small case tucked in the motor compartment has new ones, so you replace them. You tighten screws, replace fuses, and use a bottle of oil to lube various parts. You even find a can of gasoline that you add to the motor's tank. You started out just guessing, but it seems you have a knack for this.

You try to start the motor again. This time, it makes a deeper noise before sputtering out. You give it one more try. *VROOOOOOOM!* The motor starts! For a few minutes, gray smoke wafts out of the motor compartment, but that disappears as the motor gets fresh gasoline.

You shout, "Woo-hoo!" at the top of your lungs and put the boat into gear. It jolts to life. You're actually moving!

You don't know which direction to go, or how far your fuel will get you. You know there are lots of islands in the South Pacific, so you head southwest.

After a few hours, you see something—a large cargo ship. You steer the boat straight for it, pulling up alongside. A few of the ship's crew peer at you over the railing.

"Need some help, mate?" one of them calls.

You let out a huge sigh. Your ordeal is over. It's time to go home.

THE END

To follow another path, turn to page 9.
To learn more about survival at sea, turn to page 101.

You slump to the deck. "I give up," you mumble out loud. "I can't do anything right."

It's a turning point in your journey. You're lonely and defeated. You keep yourself alive, but all your hope of finding rescue is gone.

The days go on. Eventually, another dry spell and dehydration get the best of you. You survived for months at sea with almost no resources. But it couldn't go on forever, and now your ordeal is at an end.

THE END

To follow another path, turn to page 9.
To learn more about survival at sea, turn to page 101.

Staying positive is a big part of survival. You'll just have to try again. This time, you use a tattered tarp from back in the engine compartment. It's smaller than the sheet, but it's better than nothing. You're almost surprised when the wind catches it. It's working—not very well, but it's working.

You let the winds carry you for another week. Then, finally, you spot land. An island! As you get closer, you can see buildings along the shore and a marina filled with other boats!

You can barely believe your eyes. After months at sea hoping for rescue, you've taken matters into your own hands. No one was coming to save you. So you kept working and saved yourself. You can't wait to tell your friends and family all about it.

THE END

To follow another path, turn to page 9.
To learn more about survival at sea, turn to page 101.

CHAPTER 5

A WATER WORLD

Oceans cover more than seventy percent of Earth's surface. Many places on the ocean's surface are hundreds of miles from land. Huge stretches of water can be far from the paths commonly used by ships and airplanes. Someone lost in one of these vast, remote ocean areas faces serious challenges.

The oceans also drive much of Earth's weather. Strong storms get their energy from warm ocean waters. Winds can kick up huge waves. Currents can drag ships far off course.

So what should someone do if they find themselves lost at sea? That depends on many factors. Are they aboard a damaged boat or ship? Have they been tossed to the sea in a raft or other small craft? How far away is land?

In most cases, drinking water is the first priority. A person lost at sea is surrounded by water. But the oceans are made of saltwater. Drinking it is deadly. For someone who is desperately thirsty, the temptation to drink ocean water can be overpowering. But the high salt content will only speed up dehydration.

Collecting rainwater is the key to surviving if you have no fresh water on hand. Use items like tarps or empty containers to catch and store it. In a pinch, it's even okay to drink urine. But be careful. As a person drinks urine, toxins build up in the body. It's a strategy to use only as a last resort.

In tropical areas, the sun can create a problem. When the body overheats, a deadly condition called heatstroke can set in. Baking in the hot sun also speeds up dehydration. Any shade can be a lifesaver. Taking shelter under tarps or even extra clothes during the midday hours can make all the difference.

The sea can offer plenty of food—if one has the ability to catch it. Fishing gear on a boat or ship could be crucial. Fish are rich in fats and proteins that help fuel the body. Some survivors catch and eat sea birds. In a survival situation, you can't be picky.

Rescue is the biggest goal. Ships regularly cross many parts of the ocean. Flares and flashlights can help signal these ships. Even waving brightly colored fabric can be helpful.

Any sign that shows you need help is a plus. You could paint SOS—an international distress call—on the side of a boat or spell it out with rocks if you're stuck on an island.

Sometimes, people lost at sea must rescue themselves. Use anything you can to make a sail. The more you move, the better your chance of finding dry land. And if you do spot it, do everything you can to reach it.

Being lost at sea is a life-threatening situation. But with a little luck and the will to survive, you just might make it out alive.

TRUE LOST AT SEA SURVIVAL STORIES

LOUIS ZAMPERINI AND RUSSELL PHILLIPS

LOUIS ZAMPERINI

In 1943, Louis Zamperini, Russell Phillips, and Francis McNamara were serving in the U.S. Army Air Forces during World War II (1939–1945) when their plane went down in the Pacific Ocean. Of the eleven men onboard, only those three survived the crash. They climbed onto a pair of small life rafts. The three men survived on rainwater, sea birds, and what fish they could catch. Zamperini even killed a shark and ate its liver. McNamara died after thirty-three days. After forty-seven days at sea, Zamperini and Phillips came ashore on the Marshall Islands. They were taken prisoner by the Japanese military and sent to prison camps. Both survived and returned home after the war.

TAMI OLDHAM ASHCRAFT

In 1983, Tami Oldham Ashcraft and Richard Sharp were sailing from Tahiti to San Diego, California, on a yacht. Twenty days into their voyage, they ran into a hurricane. The violent waves slammed the yacht. Sharp was washed out to sea. Ashcraft was knocked unconscious but survived the storm. She made a small sail and used the sun to navigate. After forty-one days alone at sea, she managed to guide the yacht to Hawaii.

JOSÉ SALVADOR ALVARENGA

Salvadorian fisherman José Salvador Alvarenga survived fourteen months lost at sea aboard a small fishing boat. He and Ezequiel Córdoba went out on a fishing trip in November 2012. A storm blew them off course and damaged the boat's motor. Córdoba died of starvation, but Alvarenga kept going. In January 2014, he spotted land. Alvarenga swam to a small island, where he found people.

107

S.T.O.P. TO SURVIVE

The best way to remember what to do if you find yourself in an emergency situation is to S.T.O.P. Each letter stands for an instruction you can follow to help get yourself to safety.

S.T.O.P.: Stop, Think, Observe, Plan

Stop: Stay calm and take in the situation.

Think: What do you need to do to survive? What supplies do you have on hand that you could use?

Observe: Look around. Do you see familiar landmarks? Can you tell what direction you're pointed?

Plan: Make a plan of action and never give up.

OTHER PATHS TO EXPLORE

1. Imagine finding someone who had been lost at sea. Maybe you spotted them from a boat or an aircraft. Or maybe you saw them as they stumbled to shore after finally finding dry land. What would you say to someone in that situation? How would you offer immediate help? And where would you take them?

2. What would it be like to have a family member who was lost at sea? Would you hold out hope that they were alive? Would you have a funeral if you thought they had died? And then what might it be like to hear the news that they survived and are on their way home?

3. Often, search and rescue missions are sent out for people who are lost at sea. What would it be like to be a part of those missions? Looking for a small boat on the vast ocean can be like looking for a needle in a haystack. Would you have what it takes to be a part of the search team? How would you stay positive in such a stressful job?

GLOSSARY

capsize (KAP-syz)—to tip over in the water

cockpit (KOK-pit)—the area in the front of a plane where the pilot sits

current (KUHR-uhnt)—the movement of water in a river or an ocean

dehydration (dee-hy-DRAY-shuhn)—a life-threatening medical condition caused by a lack of water

hull (HUHL)—the main body of a boat

rudder (RUHD-ur)—a flat handle at the back of a boat used for steering

tropical (TRAH-pi-kuhl)—having to do with the hot and wet areas near the equator

yacht (YOT)—a large boat or small ship used for sailing or racing

READ MORE

Bell, Samantha. *Being Lost at Sea*. New York: AV2l, 2020.

Lassieur, Allison. *Can You Survive Death-defying Ocean Encounters?: An Interactive Wilderness Adventure*. North Mankato, MN: Capstone, 2023.

Yomtov, Nel. *The Unbreakable Zamperini: A World War II Survivor's Brave Story*. North Mankato, MN: Capstone, 2020.

INTERNET SITES

9 Unbelievable True Stories About People Who Survived Being Lost at Sea
popularmechanics.com/adventure/g2770/lost-at-sea/

Ocean Habitats
kids.nationalgeographic.com/nature/habitats/article/ocean

Stranded at Sea? Follow this 7-Step Extreme Survival Guide
cnn.com/2013/04/11/sport/ultimate-survival-guide/index.html

ABOUT THE AUTHOR

Matt Doeden is a freelance author and editor from Minnesota. He's written numerous children's books on sports, music, current events, the military, extreme survival, and much more. His book *It's Outta Here* was included on Bank Street's Best Books of the Year List in 2022. He lives in Minnesota with his wife and two children.